W9-AUS-356

Indian Nations

THE MENOMINEE

by
Verna Fowler

General Editors
Herman J. Viola and David Jeffery

A Rivilo Book

RAINTREE
STECK-VAUGHN
PUBLISHERS

A Harcourt Company

Austin · New York
www.steck-vaughn.com

Published by Raintree Steck-Vaughn Company, an imprint of the Steck-Vaughn Company

Developed for Steck-Vaughn Company by Rivilo Books

Editors: David Jeffery and David Stern
Photo Research: Linda Sykes
Design: Barbara Lisenby and Todd Hirshman
Electronic Preparation: Lyda Guz

Raintree Steck-Vaughn Publishers Staff
Publishing Director: Walter Kossmann
Editor: Kathy DeVico

Photo Credits: Steve Raymer/National Geographic Image Collection: cover, pp. 24, 25, 29 top, 30, 32 left, 38 top, 39, 40; Lisa Ranallo Horse Capture: illustration, pp. 4, 6; Annie Hubbard: p. 7; Tim Zurowski/Corbis: p. 8; Manitoba Museum of Man and Nature: p. 9; State Historical Society of Wisconsin: pp. 9 top Whi (x3) 50167, 11 bottom Whi (x3) no. 40974, 28 right, 34 Whi (x3) 41833; Larry Waukau: pp. 10, 38 left, 41 left; Ric Ergenbright/Corbis: p. 11 top; Milwaukee Public Museum: p. 12; Library of Congress: p. 15; Hulton Getty/Liaison International: pp. 17, 35; Corbis: pp. 18, 19; Bruce Fritz/Capital Times: p. 21 left; JP Rowan: p. 21 right; Bettmann/Corbis: p. 22; Verna Fowler: pp. 23, 31, 41 right; Courtesy President & Fellows of Harvard College Peabody Museum, Harvard University: 26 left and right, 27 top; Minnesota Historical Society: p. 27 bottom; National Anthropological Archives/Smithsonian Institution: pp. 28 bottom, 29 bottom; Verna de Leone: p. 32 right; Photo courtesy Menominee Nation News/L. Tucker: p. 33; Verna de Leone: 37 top and bottom; Royal Ontario Museum: p. 43; Lyda Guz: p. 44.

Library of Congress Cataloging-in-Publication Data
Fowler, Verna.
     The Menominee / by Verna Fowler.
       p. cm. — (Indian nations)
     Includes bibliographical references and index.
     ISBN 0-8172-5458-7
     1. Menominee Indians — History — Juvenile literature. 2. Menominee Indians — Social life and customs — Juvenile literature. [1. Menominee Indians. 2. Indians of North America — Michigan. 3. Indians of North America — Wisconsin.] I. Title. II. Series: Indian nations (Austin, Tex.)
E99.M44 F68   2001
977.4004'973—dc21

00-034161

Printed and bound in the United States
1 2 3 4 5 6 7 8 9 0 LB 04 03 02 01 00

Cover photo: A Menominee girl holds her pet rabbit.

Contents

Creation Story. 5

Manabush and the Dancing Birds. 7

Key Historical Events. 9

Way of Life 23

Spiritual Life 29

Family Life 31

Tribal Government 34

Contemporary Life 36

Menominee Prayer. 42

Menominee Recipes 43

Menominee Chronology 45

Glossary 46

Further Reading 47

Sources. 47

Index 48

Pronunciation of some Menominee words are found in the Glossary.

Creation Story

Menominee stories and legends were used to teach or to entertain. The stories instructed children how to behave, taught a moral, or explained the world around them. As entertainment, they were told around the campfire as bedtime stories. The Menominee Creation Story explains how the world of the Menominee began.

Maeq-Awaetok (Great Spirit) made the Sun, the stars, and the Earth. Mother Earth gave birth to Keso (the Moon). Then the Moon gave birth to twins, whose work was to finish the creation of the world. Before the people came into the world, the land, rivers, mountains, and lakes were formed. After the plants and animals and other living things had all been made, a great bear with a copper tail arose from the ground beside the Menominee River. As the bear explored the land on which he lived, the Great Spirit changed him into a person. This bear became the first Menominee.

Walking along the river, the bear noticed an eagle flying in the sky. He called out to the eagle, saying, "Come and join me and be my brother." As the bird flew down, the Great Spirit changed him into a Menominee as well.

The two brothers, bear and eagle, continued on their journey. In turn, they came upon the beaver, sturgeon, elk, crane, wolf, dog, and deer. All of them were changed into human beings as well, becoming members of the Menominee tribe.

◄ *The twin children of the Moon created the animals.*
Then the Great Spirit changed those animals into people.
They became the first spiritual ancestors of the Menominee.

The bear and eagle were the elder brothers and formed the tribe's major groups, or **clans**. The earliest Menominee chiefs came from the Bear clan, while the great warriors came out of the Eagle clan.

The Menominee believed that land, like the air, could not be owned. They believed that the land was their mother. She gave them all they needed to live. The land, air, water, plants, and animals were there for them to use. However, they had to use all of those gifts very carefully so that they would be there for the people born in the future.

Manabush and the Dancing Birds

Manabush is an important character in many Menominee tales and legends. The Menominee believed he was sent to Earth by the Great Spirit, Maeq-Awaetok, to teach them how to live in peace with each other and with the animals. Manabush showed the Menominee how to use fire to keep them warm, find plants as medicine for healing, and taught them how to hunt and be great warriors.

One day Manabush was returning home after a long journey. He was very tired and hungry. As he walked along the lakeshore, he saw a large flock of swans and ducks swimming. One of the swans called out, "Ho, Manabush! Where are you going?"

Seeing the birds, Manabush decided that they would make a very tasty evening meal.

"I am going to sing a song," he answered. "My brothers, come ashore, and let us sing and dance together." The birds agreed. Manabush then took his singing stick and drum and said, "Now all of you dance around me and sing with me as loudly as you can. Be sure to keep your eyes closed."

With that, Manabush began to drum and sing. The birds

This artist's interpretation of the story shows Manabush playing his drum for a flock of waterbirds.

7

danced in a circle around him. But as one swan danced by, Manabush grabbed it from the circle and broke its neck. Another bird came dancing by—and again, Manabush grabbed it. This bird, however, let out a scream before dying.

Before any of the other birds had time to wonder what the sound was, Manabush began drumming even harder. "Good, my brothers!" he shouted. "Keep singing as loudly as you can!"

In this way, Manabush soon had a pile of birds for his dinner. Then one bird, the helldiver (a ducklike bird, now called a grebe), not hearing his friends singing as loudly as before, opened his eyes.

"My brothers!" the helldiver cried out. "Manabush is killing us! Fly away!"

The warning frightened the other birds, so they hurried to escape. Some flew away. Others, including the helldiver, ran toward the lake. But the helldiver was a poor runner, so Manabush caught him easily.

"I will not kill you," Manabush said. "But for your deed you will always have red eyes and be the laughingstock of all the birds!" Then, grabbing the bird by its tail, he threw him far into the lake, pulling out his tail feathers.

That is why the rings around the eyes of the helldiver are red, and why, to this day, it is without a tail.

How did this bird, now called a grebe, get his red eyes? In Menominee legend, the hero Manabush, who was sent by the Great Spirit, played tricks on birds. But one bird, the helldiver, played a trick on Manabush. To punish the helldiver, Manabush caught him, yanked out his tail feathers, and turned his eyes red forever.

Key Historical Events

The land where the great bear first became a man is at the mouth of the Menominee River. This river now forms part of the boundary between the state of Wisconsin and the Upper Peninsula of Michigan. Scientists have found evidence that people have lived along this river for at least three thousand years.

The remains of a walled settlement built of earth by prehistoric Indians is located near Wisconsin's capital, Madison. Those ancient people may have been true ancestors of the Menominee.

Some scientists believe the Menominee's ancestors were the Copper Culture people, who lived by the Great Lakes ten thousand years ago. They were given this name because they shaped copper found near Lake Superior into tools. Others believe that the Menominee may be related to the Mound Builders, who also lived in the area long ago. These people left behind huge piles of earth, some of which still remain.

The Menominee may also have been related to people of the Old Copper Culture. These people made spear points from copper, which was plentiful along the south shore of Lake Superior.

9

The Menominee themselves believe they came from the water into a land where they were brothers to the animals. Scientists know that thousands of years ago, the continents of Asia and North America were joined by a narrow bridge of land. People migrated across this bridge and settled in what is now Alaska. Slowly, they moved south in search of food and a warmer place to live. Perhaps these movements are the source for the Menominee legends.

The Menominee spoke a dialect of the Algonquian language, similar to that of the Ojibwa, Ottawa, Cree, Sac, and Kickapoo tribes. Their neighbors, the Ojibwa, called the Menominee the Mano'min ini'niw'k, or "wild rice men," after the crop that was their staple food. In their own language the Menominee called themselves **Mamaceqtaw** (ma-ma-CHAY-tua), which means "the people who live with the seasons."

Wild rice grows tall along the shores of Pine Lake, Wisconsin. When its grains ripen, Menominee people paddle canoes to the plants. Then they knock the plants with sticks to make the grain fall into their boats.

Cliffs along the shores of Lake Michigan and Lake Superior have been part of the Menominee homeland for thousands of years.

Before Christopher Columbus arrived in the Americas, the Menominee lived on almost ten million acres of land. It covered an area from what is now Michigan's Upper Peninsula south to Milwaukee, Wisconsin, and west as far as the Wisconsin River.

Meeting Jean Nicolet

In 1634 the Menominee met their first European, Jean Nicolet. He was a French fur trader on his way to the Winnebago village at Red Banks (near the present city of Green Bay, Wisconsin). Bearded and dressed in Chinese clothing, and shooting his "thunder-sticks" (pistols), Nicolet was a frightening sight. Eventually the tribe welcomed him. After Nicolet left, the Menominee had little contact with Europeans for nearly thirty years.

In 1634 the Menominee met their first European. Though he was a French fur trader, Jean Nicolet was dressed in Chinese clothing at the time of the meeting. He was a strange sight indeed!

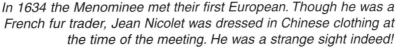

The Fur Trade

Gradually, more French traders came to the Great Lakes region, giving rise to the fur trade. That trade supplied beaver pelts, which were in great demand in Europe for fashion and for warmth. The fur trade changed the Menominee way of life forever. It changed the Indians' work habits, the places they traveled, the tools they used, the food they ate, and the clothing they wore. It also changed the way they raised and taught their children, made their arts and crafts, and expressed their spiritual beliefs.

Before the Europeans, the Menominee were hunters and fishermen with small gardens of corn, squash, and beans. They followed the seasons, moving to where food was plentiful and gathered fruits, nuts, and roots. With the fur trade they spent more time trapping beaver and other animals. They traded the animal skins for European goods such as knives, kettles, cloth, flour, coffee, sugar, and hatchets. The knives and hatchets made building their homes and canoes easier. Where once they had fashioned dugout canoes by burning out the centers of logs, they now cut planks from the logs and joined the planks together. This was faster and easier. No longer did they make birch bark containers. They used metal kettles. Nor did they

Although the Menominee traded many beaver pelts to Europeans, they also turned pelts into beautiful objects. This medicine bag, perhaps owned by a holy man, was made from a beaver pelt. It was then decorated with porcupine quills.

Trading posts on the frontier were like today's shopping malls. Europeans wanted furs, especially beaver. Indians wanted rifles, knives, axes, cloth, and foodstuffs such as flour. At the trading posts, Europeans and Indians could swap goods without using money.

have to grind corn for corn flour. They traded for wheat flour. Brightly colored cloth and ribbons replaced animal hides for clothing. As time went by, the Menominee no longer lived in shelters called **we-ke-wams**, or lodges, while moving from place to place. Instead they built log cabins and remained in one place. By doing so, they ceased to follow the seasons as much as they had earlier. However, as beavers and other animals became scarce from overhunting, Menominee hunters had to move greater distances in search of more plentiful game. In their travels, the Menominee met more Europeans and other Indians and saw new items that would make their lives easier. Once villages became established near trading posts, missionaries arrived and built schools and taught the Indians Christian beliefs.

Relations with the French and British

The French and the Menominee became friends. The French did not send families to the New World to build towns or large farms as the British did. The French were more interested in building forts and trading posts. As a result, fighting over land did not erupt as often as it had between the British and Indians on the Atlantic coast. The friendship between the French and Indians grew even stronger as fur traders began to marry Menominee women.

PRÆVALEBIT ÆQUIOR.

The English and the French vied for the loyalty of Indians in the Northeast and Great Lakes regions in the 17th and 18th centuries.

The French considered the Great Lakes area theirs until the late 1600s, when the British began to gain control. War then broke out between the French and British. The Indian tribes had to choose sides. Because of their friendship with the French, the Menominee allied with them.

In 1754 what is commonly known as the French and Indian War started. This war is misnamed. It should be called the British and French War. This war determined which country would be the most powerful in the Great Lakes area and along the Atlantic coast. It lasted for nine years before the British finally won.

The Indians in the Great Lakes area had not become as friendly with the British as they had been with the French. The British did not give them gifts of cloth, guns, canoes, and other items as the French had done. The Menominee had done some fur trading with the British, but beavers were becoming scarce. Not only was the supply low, but so was the demand. Silk was becoming the fashion in Europe.

In 1775 some British colonists along the coast of the Atlantic Ocean rebelled against their king in England and British forces in North America. So began the war known as the American Revolution. The fighting was far away from Menominee villages, and the Menominee remained loyal to the British government. But when the Revolution ended with a victory for the American rebels, the British agreed to leave the lower Great Lakes region.

However, many of them stayed and continued trading with the Indians. At the same time more former colonists, now called Americans, began moving into the area to farm on Indian lands. In 1811 Britain and the newly formed United States went to war again, because the British did not keep their promise to leave. Again, the Menominee sided with the British. But by 1815, the British were entirely driven out of the lower Great Lakes.

Relations with the United States Government

With the British and French both gone, the Menominee came under the authority of the new United States government. In 1816 the United States sent an agent to meet with the Menominee near the present-day Mackinaw Bridge in Michigan. At that meeting, the Menominee had to pledge their loyalty to the American government. This was the first of several meetings between the two sides. Future meetings were called for the purpose of signing **treaties**—formal, written agreements made between countries or governments.

The Menominee did not go to war against the United States government to save their land as did many other Indian tribes. With the establishment of five United States army forts equipped with cannons in their territory, the Menominee knew that they could be overpowered easily and defeated. To hold on to their land and stay where they were, the Menominee used stalling tactics, including the calling of meetings. This was a sort of passive resistance. The tribe would agree to have meetings with government officials. These meetings would lead to more meetings. The tribe hoped the government would get tired of the continual meetings and finally leave the tribe alone. Sometimes, though, the Menominee just refused to move.

In 1824 the United States Congress established an agency called the **Bureau of Indian Affairs** to oversee the Indian tribes in America. Because the tribes were nations that had been conquered by the United States Army, this bureau was made part of the United States War Department.

The Menominee signed seven major treaties with the United States government, the first in 1817 and the last in 1854. In these treaties the Menominee gave up about nine and one-half million acres of their homeland. In return they were promised medical care, education, and food. Sometimes salt, tobacco, blankets, farm tools, and other items were given as payment for the land. After all the treaties were signed, the Menominee were forced to live on a **reservation** of 234,000 acres (94,700 ha) in northern Wisconsin.

In 1825 the Menominee were one of eight tribes to sign a "Great Treaty" with the United States at Prairie du Chien, Wisconsin.

Reservation life was not easy for the Menominee. The area was too small for hunting and food gathering and too sandy and rocky for farming. But part of the Menominee reservation was rich with trees. Lumber barons, Americans who cut trees and milled them into lumber, wanted the United States government to let them cut the trees on the Menominee reservation. The Indians resisted. The U.S. government finally agreed that the Menominee could cut and sell the trees themselves, but only to certain selected white men. Those white men would be allowed to pay a low price for the lumber and then sell it at much higher prices to anyone they wished. Still, by 1871, the Menominee sawmill was so successful that the tribe had $10,000 saved in the United States Treasury. In 1886 the tribe built a new sawmill, which raised production to 15 million board feet of lumber a year.

In 1890 the United States government passed a new law that let the Menominee sell lumber to anyone they wished. Menominee lumber profits in the United States Treasury grew

In 1909 real horsepower brought logs cut from big trees to the sawmill on the Menominee Reservation.

to $200,000 per year. The Indians used this money to build and support schools, a hospital, and to help the poorest Indians on the reservation. In 1908 the tribe used the money they had saved to build a modern sawmill on the Wolf River in Wisconsin. A new village called Neopit formed around the mill.

Huge saw blades driven by machinery cut logs into lumber at the sawmill of the Menominee. The mill opened in Neopit, Wisconsin, in 1908. It brought income to the tribe for many years.

In 1911 a railroad was constructed through Neopit to make shipping the lumber faster and easier. With the mill profits, by 1940 the tribe had established not only a hospital and schools, but also a health clinic, a police department, a court system, and a welfare fund for the poor.

Termination and Restoration

In the 1950s, the U.S. government developed a new policy toward Native Americans. The Menominee and several other Indian tribes were among the first picked for **"Termination."** (When a life, a game, or system is terminated, that means it is ended.) They were picked because they seemed able to support themselves.

Under the Termination plan, Indians in the United States were to be treated as ordinary U.S. citizens with no special protection from their treaties. For example, as with all U.S. citizens, Native Americans would now be subject to federal and state taxes. The Bureau of Indian Affairs was to be closed, and all the treaties the Indians had signed with the government would no longer be legal. The solemn promises made long ago would no longer be kept.

In 1954 the United States Congress passed the **Menominee Termination Act**. The 234,000 acres of reservation land that the tribe owned as a group became Menominee County, the 72nd county of the state of Wisconsin.

The termination of the Menominee tribe plunged a successful people into hopeless poverty. The hospital and clinic had to be closed because they did not meet the standards set by the state. Neither the sanitation facilities nor the roads met state standards. There was no longer enough money to support the welfare fund for the poor.

The sawmill the tribe owned was made into a private corporation, or business. The sawmill's profits had to be used to pay state property taxes on the huge forest that once had been the heart of the reservation. Because the timber was valuable, the taxes were very high. The sawmill profits did not even cover taxes owed. So the sawmill managers developed a plan to sell land to get the money they needed to stay in business.

The Wolf River flows through the village of Keshena, and several lakes nearby empty into it. To get the needed money for taxes, a plan was made to build dams on the lakes, creeks, and swamplands and dig channels to join the smaller lakes into one large lake. This lake, named Legend Lake, was divided into lots for vacation home sites for sale to white people. Lake lots, totaling more than 5,000 acres (2,024 ha) of land on Legend Lake, nearby lakes, and the Wolf River were sold for development.

The loss of the land angered many of the Menominee. They formed a group called Determination of Rights and Unity for Menominee Shareholders (**DRUMS**). Their goal was to get the county turned back into a reservation and have the people recognized by the United States government as Menominee Indians once more.

From 1968 to 1970, DRUMS held protest marches to the sales offices where lake lots were being sold. Leading that effort was an activist named Ada Deer. She was the first member of the tribe to have graduated from the University of Wisconsin in

Whitewater sparkles on the Wolf River (above) as it runs through the Menominee Reservation.

In the 1970s, Menominees protested (left) against federal government policies that took away their status as an independent Indian nation.

Madison. She also earned a master's degree in social work from Columbia University—before returning to help her tribe's causes.

Besides protesting the sale of lake lots, Ms. Deer and DRUMS also worked to get the support of Wisconsin's governor, senators, and representatives in Congress. They needed that support to pressure the United States government to **repeal** the Menominee Termination Act. DRUMS also worked to get its members elected as managers of the sawmill, so that they could stop the sale of the land around Legend Lake. All their efforts finally succeeded in 1973 when President Richard Nixon signed the **Menominee Restoration Act**. This act gave the Menominee back their status as an Indian tribe and restored their reservation to tribal ownership.

Ada Deer led the struggle to have the government return the Menominee to their past way of life as a tribe.

Life after restoration was not the same as before for the Menominee. Still suffering from severe poverty, they had to elect leaders, set up a tribal government, and write a constitution. They also had to update the **tribal roll**. The tribal roll was a listing of all the names and dates of birth for living members of the tribe and their ancestors as well. In the years since, there has been much work to do in order to improve education, health care, and provide employment opportunities. The work continues.

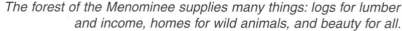

Way of Life

Indian peoples are often grouped together according to where they lived. For example, the Lakota (Sioux) Indians, along with the Cheyenne, Mandan, Hidatsa, and others are called Plains Indians because they lived on the Great Plains. The Navajo, Hopi, Zuni, and Apache lived in the desert areas of Arizona and New Mexico. They and other tribes in this area are called Southwestern Indians.

Tribes are grouped this way because living in similar areas led them to develop similar cultures. Their physical environments shaped the way they built their homes, the way they dressed, the foods they ate, the arts and crafts they created, and to some degree their spiritual beliefs.

The land in which the Menominee lived was mostly forest. Thus, the Menominee, Ojibwa, Ottawa, Huron, Mohawk, and

The forest of the Menominee supplies many things: logs for lumber and income, homes for wild animals, and beauty for all.

their neighbors are called Woodland Indians. The Menominee were part of the Eastern Woodland culture covering the area roughly south from Minnesota to below the Ohio River and east to the Atlantic Ocean. Tribes of this culture lived mostly by hunting, fishing, food gathering, and growing small crops of corn, squash, and beans.

Food

The Menominee found many different kinds of food in the woodlands. Their varied diet gave them the vitamins and minerals they needed to be healthy and strong. From the rivers and lakes they took fish, spearing them from a canoe or riverbank, or using **weirs** (fixed nets) to catch them. They held a feast

Grinning children hold pelts from raccoons their father trapped. The pelts brought extra income to the family.

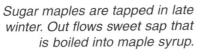

celebrating the return of huge fish called sturgeon, which migrated upriver each spring. Lake Michigan and smaller lakes, rivers, and streams held many other kinds of fish, including trout, bass, crappie, walleye, perch, and whitefish.

Forests and prairies provided abundant wild game. The Menominee hunted as a group for larger animals such as bear, deer, moose, and buffalo. To catch smaller game, such as rabbits, squirrels, beaver, and porcupine, the tribe used various types of traps and snares. Migrating birds and waterfowl were also part of the Menominee diet.

Not everyone left the village to hunt. Children and the elderly stayed behind to tend the tribe's gardens of beans, corn, and squash. The Menominee also gathered wild berries and fruits, such as apples, to add to their diet.

Everyone helped to gather the tribe's main food, wild rice. Adults paddled among its stalks in canoes, knocking the ripe grain into their boats. Once brought ashore, the rice was placed on animal skins in a hole. The children then pounded or danced on the rice to separate the outer covering, or chaff, which was not good to eat, from the grain that was.

The tribe also collected sap from the maple trees in their forests. They made the sap into maple syrup and used it to flavor food. When the syrup hardened, it could be eaten as a candy treat.

Sugar maples are tapped in late winter. Out flows sweet sap that is boiled into maple syrup.

Clothing

The Menominee made clothing from animal skins. Mostly they used deerskin. Before the skins could be worn, they were tanned, a process that made them soft. Then the deer hair was scraped off, and juices of different plants were used to dye the skin.

Robes, with the fur of the deer left on, provided protection from wind and cold. Animals also provided material for making hats, robes, footwear, leggings, and blankets. Women decorated clothing with shells or dyed porcupine quills. With the coming of the French, European cloth was used and sometimes sewed in fancy patterns and decorated with colorful ribbons.

Old and new styles of weapons and clothing were mixed long ago. A man holds a rifle and war club (left). A woman's dress (right) is decorated with glass beads that first came from Europe.

Houses

The Menominee did not live in tipis as the Plains Indians did. Their homes were lodges called we-ke-wams. Different types were used according to the seasons. In winter, the lodges were dome-shaped, made by bending saplings (young trees) into a half circle about six feet tall, tying them together, and covering them with mats made of birch bark. The birch bark was stripped and woven with strips of ash into larger pieces and tied to the sapling frames.

In summer, the lodges were rectangular, made by constructing a frame of peeled logs. These structures changed little until the 19th century, when the Menominee adopted one-room log homes and buildings constructed of lumber.

In the old days, winter lodges called we-ke-wams (right) were made of saplings and birch bark. Today, houses are sometimes made of logs as they were in the 1800s (below), while others are built with frames and siding.

Arts and Crafts

The Menominee took great pride in decorating their clothing with elaborate geometric patterns. They originally used shell ornaments, feathers, and dyed porcupine quills to do this. The clothing was beautiful, but it took a long time to do all the leather tanning, quill dyeing, and stitching. In the 17th century Europeans introduced the Menominee to glass beads, cloth fabric, ribbons, and other manufactured objects. Where the Menominee had once used quills to decorate deerskin clothing, they now began to decorate cloth with complex beadwork patterns that often looked like flowers. They also made fine baskets from local grasses and the wood of young trees.

Bags decorated with beads (right) replaced those that were made from dyed porcupine quills.

Early in the 20th century, Menominees, like this man and woman (below), made baskets of wood and grass, beadwork of glass, and snowshoes from bent wood and woven rawhide.

Spiritual Life

The Menominee, like all Indian people, were a spiritual or religious people. They used prayer, dance, offerings, and songs to show honor, respect, and give thanks to the spirits. The Menominee believed that it was Manabush who left them instructions for their religious ceremonies.

Religious leaders called shamans knew the prayers and rites and conducted services. They also knew how to talk with the spirits. Before any major undertaking, such as hunting, harvesting, planting, going on a journey, or going to war, the spirits were asked for help. Fear of spirits was a major belief, so the Menominee always tried to please them.

The Menominee always took time to pray to the spirits to thank them for favors and to ask for their help. While other plants were taken for food or as medicine, tobacco was left to offer thanks. Before a canoe trip or

Menominees now dance in powwows (above). Long ago, they held ceremonies in special lodges (below) built for religious celebrations.

before harvesting wild rice, tobacco was thrown on the water to give thanks and to ask for safe travel or a rich harvest. Tobacco was left at grave sites as a gift for the spirits or sprinkled about for safety from approaching storms. The tribe also used prayer, songs, and dances such as the War Dance to honor the spirits.

Menominee religious ideas were changed by French Roman Catholic priests who followed behind the early fur traders. In 1669 Father Claude Allouez began establishing missions among the Menominee. Later, schools were added to educate the Indians and teach them the Roman Catholic faith. Today, most Menominee consider themselves Catholics, although various other Christian sects also have followers. Some sects are Indian in origin, such as the Native American Church, the Big Drum Religion, and Midewin.

Today, Menominee men and women are often married in Christian ceremonies and wear the same kind of wedding dress that most other Americans do. Many Menominee are able to blend their traditional culture with that of the modern world.

Family Life

The Family

Families in American society today are usually referred to as "**nuclear families**." A nuclear family consists of two parents and their children. Indian tribes had extended families. An **extended family** includes the nuclear family with one or more close relatives, such as grandparents or aunts and uncles. In extended families, all share the work and the benefits of the work. Raising children was everyone's responsibility. Menominee grandparents watched children when parents went off to hunt, gather food, harvest wild rice, or fish.

Children were not generally spanked or loudly scolded. Rather, fear and shame were used to teach them how to act. Children were told that a ghost or spirit would take them away

Author Verna Fowler's kin gather for a reunion. She is in the middle, wearing glasses, behind the woman holding a dog. This family group is only one-fourth of Dr. Fowler's entire extended family.

A man carries a young black bear whose pelt is valuable. Menominees may hunt, trap, and fish at any time on their land, but they do not kill just for sport.

if they behaved badly. Or, they were told not to shame or embarrass the family, clan, or tribe by their behavior.

The Menominee lived in villages of small groups called **bands**. This arrangement saved or conserved the plants and animals in an area. In the summer and fall, men hunted, fished, and trapped for meat. What families did not eat at once was dried and stored for the winter. The women gathered berries, nuts, and roots for winter storage. They also wove mats and tanned hides to make clothing and moccasins.

The Clans

Clan members were generally relatives with a common ancestor. Ancestors were traced to a spiritual being, usually an animal. All families belonged to a clan. Family members were required to work and bring wealth and honor to the clan. The power of the clan shaped correct behavior, since no one wanted to bring shame or embarrassment to the clan or the family.

There were five main clans in the Menominee tribe: Bear, Eagle (Thunderer),

Menominee artist James Frechette, Jr. stands by a giant bear that he carved. The bear represents the animal who became the first Menominee human.

Wolf, Crane, and Moose, which were in turn divided into 34 smaller groups. Each clan had certain jobs to do. Those in the Eagle clan were protectors, similar to modern-day policemen. During peacetime the leaders were from the Bear clan. During wartime, the leaders were from the Eagle clan.

Games

The Menominee, like other Indian tribes, played many different kinds of games. They used dice made of pieces of deer antlers to gamble with. Shells and stones were used as pieces for different kinds of guessing games. Lacrosse and a type of ball game using a tightly wrapped deerskin were also popular. Footraces were another form of entertainment. Singing and dancing were also used for enjoyment and social events.

In the winter, when the work slowed down, families stayed mostly in the lodges for warmth, although some hunting and fishing could be done. Evenings were spent making or mending nets, arrows, clothing, or baskets, and stories of hunting, of Manabush, or other adventures were shared.

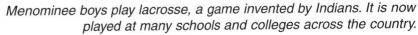

Menominee boys play lacrosse, a game invented by Indians. It is now played at many schools and colleges across the country.

Tribal Government

The Menominee did not have one main chief. The various bands each picked their own leader. The leaders were from the Bear clan or, if the tribe was at war, from the Eagle clan. Leaders were given respect but had to live up to and earn that respect. Their role was to learn the wishes of the people and make decisions based on what the people wanted.

The great leaders of the Menominee were not leaders in war as in many other Indian tribes. Menominee leaders, or chiefs, were respected and honored because they were wise in dealing with the Americans and managed to save some of the Menominee land.

One chief, Cha-wa-non, is noted because he refused to sign the first treaty with the United States. Another, Chief Tomah, is known for refusing to join with the Shawnee chief Tecumseh to drive the Americans out of the Great Lakes area. Chief Tomah did not think that going to war would solve the problem.

Chief Oshkosh, the grandchild of Cha-wa-non, is known for his wise dealings with the American government. Oshkosh, the Brave, as he was known, was not selected as tribal leader by the Menominee but was named Chief by territorial governor Lewis Cass. Oshkosh's stubborn refusal to

Chief Oshkosh, shown here in 1827, helped save the Menominee's ancient lands.

34

move the tribe to Minnesota kept the Menominee reservation on their ancestral land.

A modern leader honored by the Menominee Tribe is Ada Deer. Ms. Deer is known for working to get the Menominee people recognized as an Indian tribe by the United States government. With DRUMS, she helped to save the Menominee Reservation land from being sold by pushing for the passage of the Menominee Restoration Act. She became the tribe's chairperson and later the first woman to head the Bureau of Indian Affairs in Washington, D.C.

When the Menominee Restoration Act was passed, a new tribal government was set up with nine legislators. All enrolled members are eligible to vote for legislators, and one of them is chosen the chairperson. The government now employs over 300 people in nearly 40 different departments, including Conservation, Education, Recreation, Finance, Public Relations, Management Information Systems, and Cultural Preservation.

After she helped save the Menominee Reservation, Ada Deer was appointed to the highest post in the Bureau of Indian Affairs in Washington, D.C.

Contemporary Life

When Frenchman Jean Nicolet met the Menominee, the tribe consisted of some 800 to 1,000 members. Today, the Menominee number nearly 8,000 people, about half of whom live in the reservation's five main villages: Zoar, South Branch, Middle Village, Neopit, and Keshena.

The two outlying villages, South Branch and Zoar, consist of homes, a convenience store, a church, and a community building. Middle Village is a new settlement. It was built in 1992 to provide homes for the Menominee who have come back from cities and

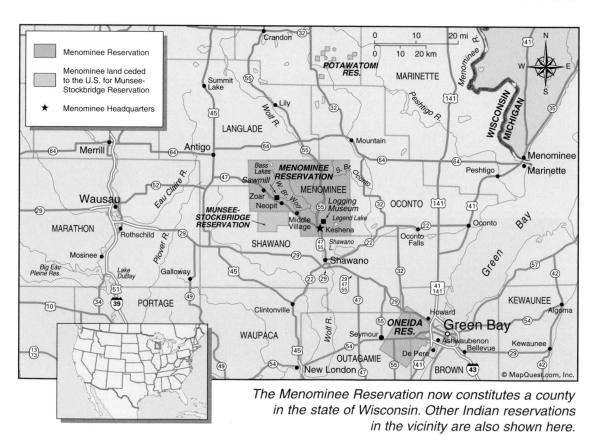

The Menominee Reservation now constitutes a county in the state of Wisconsin. Other Indian reservations in the vicinity are also shown here.

The College of Menominee Nation, opened in 1992, is in Keshena.

towns to live on the reservation. It has a drug abuse facility as well as a home for the elderly.

Neopit is the site of the sawmill, two small convenience stores, a Catholic church, the tribal elementary school, and the public middle school. Neopit has no room for future growth, since a rock ledge surrounds it.

The tribal government is headquartered in Keshena. This village also has several large office buildings, a hotel, the College of Menominee Nation, a primary school, a high school, a Catholic church, and two convenience stores.

In 1983, the Menominee opened a bingo hall in Keshena. The hall is still in operation today, along with two casinos and a 100-room hotel. All provide money to help support the tribe and its people.

Education

The Menominee have two separate school systems. One, the Menominee Tribal School, a Bureau of Indian Affairs grant school in Neopit, enrolls children from kindergarten through

Young children in a Headstart class may later go to a regular public school or to a special tribal school.

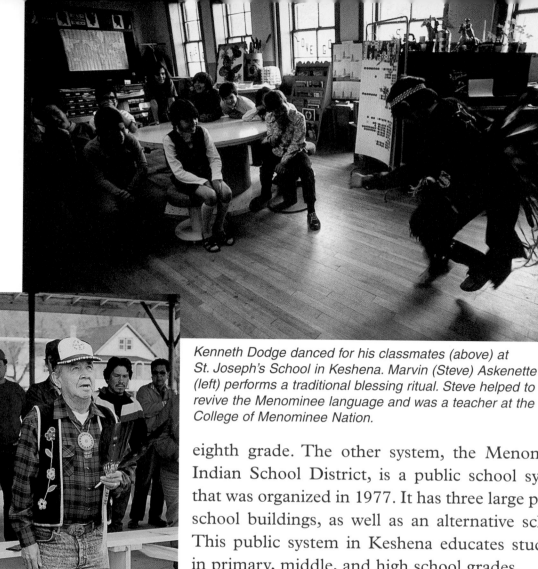

Kenneth Dodge danced for his classmates (above) at St. Joseph's School in Keshena. Marvin (Steve) Askenette (left) performs a traditional blessing ritual. Steve helped to revive the Menominee language and was a teacher at the College of Menominee Nation.

eighth grade. The other system, the Menominee Indian School District, is a public school system that was organized in 1977. It has three large public school buildings, as well as an alternative school. This public system in Keshena educates students in primary, middle, and high school grades.

In 1992 the College of Menominee Nation opened. It is a two-year college, serving more than 600 students, both Indian and non-Indian. These students take technical classes or college courses that can be transferred to Wisconsin's four-year state colleges or universities.

Economic Development

The Menominee sawmill is still operating today, shipping lumber all over the world. The sawmill provides jobs for nearly 300 men and women from the tribe and surrounding area.

Rather than sell lumber for others to make into furniture or wood products, the Menominee are now building a factory to make their own wood products. This would create more jobs and bring more money into the reservation.

Tourism is another area of economic opportunity for the Menominee. The reservation is one of the few areas in the country where one can experience a hardwood forest in its nearly original natural beauty. In addition, Legend Lake is available to tourists for boating, swimming, and fishing. The tribe also has a Logging Museum that is the largest of its kind in the world. The casino and rafting on the Wolf River also draw tourists to the region.

The sawmill of the Menominee in Neopit remains the largest industry and income-producer.

Besides the sawmill and tourism, there is little economic development on the reservation. Most Menominee must drive to Keshena to work at the government offices, the casino/hotel, clinic, or schools. People do not have the money to start a company or business. Because the reservation is so far from any large cities, other businesses do not want to build there. Shipping of goods would be too expensive. Businesses also need land and skilled workers. Both are scarce on the reservation. For shopping and entertainment, such as movies or dining out, the Menominee must drive to surrounding cities and towns.

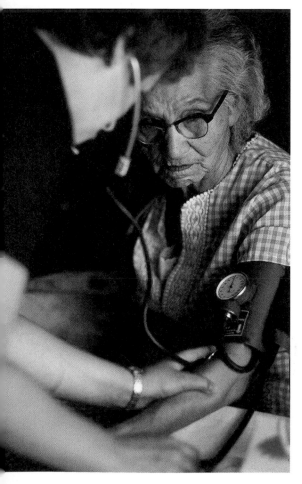

The average income on the reservation is low, and the people are poor. Because of a poor diet, many suffer from health problems, especially diabetes. The tribe also faces many of the social problems that other communities are trying to solve—gangs, drugs, and alcoholism. But progress has been made. In 1977, the Menominee became the first Indian tribe in the United States to own and operate its own medical clinic. This clinic takes care of the health needs of the Menominee and white people of the area.

Both young and old, both Menominee and non-Menominee, are welcome for treatment at the clinic owned by the tribe. It is a first line of defense against diseases such as diabetes.

The Future

The Menominee are committed to remaining true to their heritage and culture. They are proud of their accomplishments in keeping their land, forest, and waters pure and in their natural state. They plan to preserve them for future generations, to enjoy the beauty of the reservation, and to live in peace.

MENOMINEE INDIAN RESERVATION
OVER 140 YEARS OF
SUSTAINABLE FOREST MANAGEMENT

"Maeqtekuahkihkiah Kew Kanahwihtahquaq"
The Forest Keepers

• 1995 United Nations Recognition-Forest Management
• 1996 Presidential Award-Sustainable Development
• 1997 State Of Wisconsin Citation-Sustainable Forestry

Managed By Menominee Tribal Enterprises

The sign (above) says it all; the forest is all to the Menominee. They are its harvesters and protectors.

If the forest is quiet, and the rivers speak, then Smoky Falls (left) roars with delight. The ancient land is Menominee again and will be forever.

Menominee Prayer

Father of all

O Great Spirit

I'd like to pray to the Father for everyone

Thank you I say, Father, for everything

Help me to do what is right

Thank you

Great Spirit

That is all.

Menominee Recipes

Preparing Wild Rice

Adult supervision is required.

1 cup wild rice
3 cups water
1 teaspoon salt (optional)
1 bouillon cube, beef or chicken
 (optional)
(Note: Naturally grown wild rice is
green in color. Black wild rice has
been farmed or is paddy rice.)

*Naturally grown wild rice and
harvesting sticks*

Rinse the rice three times with hot water from the faucet;
then drain it. Put all the ingredients in a saucepan to boil. When
the water begins to boil, cover the pan, and lower the heat. Let
the rice simmer until the water is absorbed by the rice. This will
take about 15 to 20 minutes. The rice should be tender. It
should not burst open and look like small popcorn.

(Note: One cup of uncooked wild rice will make about 3 cups
of cooked wild rice.)

Popped Wild Rice

Adult supervision is required.

1/4 cup wild rice
1 tablespoon of vegetable oil

Rinse the wild rice thoroughly, several times. Let it dry on a towel, or put it in a warm oven for a short time. Heat the oil in a pot to 375°F. Drop the rice by large spoonfuls into the oil. Hold the pot over the heat, and shake until all the rice pops. Drain on a towel. Salt lightly. When done, the rice will look like puffed wheat cereal.

Popped wild rice

Menominee Chronology

1634	First contact with European culture. Frenchman Jean Nicolet lands at Red Banks (Wisconsin).
1669	Father Claude Allouez establishes the first mission to the Menominee near Oconto (Wisconsin).
1671	The French claim the lands in the Great Lakes area.
1754	The French and Indian War begins.
1775	The colonists rebel against England.
1811	Tecumseh tries to unite the Indians to drive out the settlers.
1817	The first Menominee treaty is signed in St. Louis.
1854	The sixth Menominee treaty is signed, defining the present reservation area.
1887	The Allotment Act (also called the Dawes Act) is passed by the U.S. Congress. Reservation land was to be divided into small parcels for each Indian family to farm. The Menominee refused to accept this act, which kept their land from being divided up and sold.
1908	A sawmill is built in Neopit.
1954	The Menominee Termination Act is passed by Congress.
1973	The Menominee Termination Act is repealed.
1977	The Menominee Tribal Clinic, the first medical clinic owned and operated by Indians in the United States, is built.
1977	The Menominee Indian School District is established.
1977	The Menominee powwow is revived.
1979	The first Menominee Tribal Legislature is elected.
1989	The first Indian gambling casino in the U.S. is established.
1991	The Menominee Tribal School is established.
1992	The College of Menominee Nation is opened.
1993	The traditional sturgeon ceremony is revived.

Glossary

Band A small group of people, usually relatives, who lived together in a village.

Bureau of Indian Affairs The agency that carries out U.S. government laws, treaties, and policies related to American Indians.

Clan A group of people related to each other because of the job or role expected of them.

DRUMS Determination for Rights and Unity for Menominee Shareholders, a Menominee group that brought the U.S. government Termination plan for American Indians to an end and saved Menominee land.

Extended family A family that includes the nuclear family and one or more close relatives.

Maeq-Awaetok (ma-jen-a-WAY-tuck) A Menominee word meaning "the Great Spirit."

Mamaceqtaw (ma-ma-CHAY-tua) The Menominee name for themselves. It means "the people who live with the seasons."

Manabush (MET-na-puss) A Menominee folk hero.

Menominee Restoration Act A U.S. government law passed in 1972. It gave back to the Menominee their reservation and identity as American Indians.

Menominee Termination Act The U.S. government law passed in 1954 that ended the Menominee's reservation and their identity as American Indians.

Nuclear family A family consisting of two parents and children.

Repeal To withdraw or take back.

Reservation Land set aside by the government for military bases or for American Indians.

Termination The ending of something.

Treaty A written agreement made by two sides or nations.

Tribal roll A listing of a tribe's members that includes their names, dates of birth, and ancestors.

Weirs Stationary nets for catching fish.

We-ke-wam (weh-keh-wahm) Menominee lodge.

Further Reading

Ourada, Patricia, and Porter, Frank W. *The Menominee.* New York: Chelsea House, 1990.

Spindler, George. *Dreamers with Power: The Menominee.* Prospect Heights, IL: Waveland Press, 1984.

Viola, Herman J. *North American Indians: An Introduction to the Lives of America's Native Peoples, from the Inuit of the Arctic to the Zuni of the Southwest.* New York: Crown Publishers, 1996.

Wood, Douglas. *Northwoods Cradle Song: From a Menominee Lullaby.* New York: Simon & Schuster, 1996.

Sources

Keesing, Felix. *The Menomini Indians of Wisconsin: A Study of Three Centuries of Cultural Contact and Change.* Philadelphia: American Philosophical Society, 1939.

Ourada, Patricia. *The Menominee Indians: A History.* Oklahoma: University of Oklahoma Press, 1979.

Ourada, Patricia, and Porter, Frank W. *The Menominee.* New York: Chelsea House, 1990.

Ritzenthaler, Robert E., and Pat Ritzenthaler. *The Woodland Indians of the Western Great Lakes.* Milwaukee Public Museum, 1983.

Shames, Deborah, Editor. *Freedom with Reservation: The Menominee Struggle to Save Their Land and People.* National Committee to Save the Menominee People and Forests, 1972.

Spindler, George, and Louise Spindler. *Dreamers with Power.* Prospect Heights, IL: Waveland Press, 1971.

Index

Numbers in italics indicate illustration or map.

Algonquian 10
Allouez, Father Claude 30
American Revolution 15
Arts and crafts 28

British 13, 14, 15, 16
Bureau of Indian Affairs 16, 20, 35, 37

Chief Cha-wa-non 34
Chief Oshkosh *34*
Chief Tomah 34
Clans 6, 32, 33, 34
Clothing *26*, 28
College of Menominee Nation *37*, 38
Copper Culture 9

Deer, Ada 21, *22*, 35
DRUMS 21, 22, 35

Economic development 38, 39, 40
Education 37, 38
European 11, 12, 13, 26, 28

Families *31*, 32
Fish 24, 25
Frechette, James Jr. *32*
French 11, 12, 13, 14, 15, 16, 26
French and Indian War 15

Great Lakes 9, 12, 15, 16, 34
Great Spirit 5, 7, 8
"Great Treaty" *17*

Keshena 20, *36*, 37, 38, 40

Lacrosse *33*
Lake Superior 9, *11*
Legend Lake 20, 21, 22, 39
Lumber 17, *18*, 19, *23*, 27, 38–39

Mamaceqtaw 10
Manabush *7*, 8, 29, 33
Medicine bag *12*
Menominee River 9
Menominee Restoration Act 22, 35
Menominee Termination Act 20, 22
Middle Village *36*

Neopit 19, *36*, 37, *39*
Nicolet, Jean *11*, 36

Plains Indians 23

Reservation 17

Sawmill *18*, *19*, 20, 22, 38, *39*
Schools *37*, 38

Shamans 29
Social problems 40
South Branch *36*
Southwestern Indians 23
Sugar maple *25*

Termination 19, 20
Trading posts *13*
Tribal government 34–35, 37

United States 15, 16, 17, 18, 19, 20, 21, 22, 35

Villages 32, *36*

Weirs 24
We-ke-wams 13, *27*
Wild game 25
Wild rice *10*, 25, 30
Wisconsin 9, *11*, 17, 19, 20
Wolf River 19, 20, *21*, 39
Woodland Indians 24

Zoar *36*